Gardening for Kids

Growing Fruits, Vegetables, and Green Thumbs in Young Gardeners

© Copyright 2024 - All rights reserved.

The content contained within this book may not be reproduced, duplicated, or transmitted without direct written permission from the author or the publisher.

Under no circumstances will any blame or legal responsibility be held against the publisher or author for any damages, reparation, or monetary loss due to the information contained within this book, either directly or indirectly.

Legal Notice:

This book is copyright-protected. It is only for personal use. You cannot amend, distribute, sell, use, quote, or paraphrase any part of the content within this book without the consent of the author or publisher.

Disclaimer Notice:

Please note the information contained within this document is for educational and entertainment purposes only. All effort has been executed to present accurate, up-to-date, reliable, and complete information. No warranties of any kind are declared or implied. Readers acknowledge that the author is not engaging in the rendering of legal, financial, medical, or professional advice. The content within this book has been derived from various sources. Please consult a licensed professional before attempting any techniques outlined in this book.

By reading this document, the reader agrees that under no circumstances is the author responsible for any losses, direct or indirect, that are incurred as a result of the use of the information contained within this document, including, but not limited to, errors, omissions, or inaccuracies.

Table of Contents

INTRODUCTION LETTER TO PARENTS 1
INTRODUCTION LETTER TO CHILDREN 3
CHAPTER ONE: GARDEN BASICS 5
CHAPTER TWO: TOOLS YOU'LL NEED 12
CHAPTER THREE: FRUITS AND VEGETABLES 19
CHAPTER FOUR: HERBS AND FLOWERS 28
CHAPTER FIVE: HARVEST TIME 36
CHAPTER SIX: GARDEN FRIENDS AND PESTS 41
CHAPTER SEVEN: TIPS AND TROUBLESHOOTING 49
CHAPTER EIGHT: FUN GARDEN PROJECTS 57
THANK YOU MESSAGE 64
HERE'S ANOTHER BOOK BY DION ROSSER THAT YOU MIGHT LIKE 65
REFERENCES 66

Introduction Letter to Parents

Dear Parents,

In today's fast-paced society, where screens dominate children's attention, it has become increasingly important to reconnect with nature and instill a love for the outdoors. Gardening provides the perfect opportunity to do just that. Not only does it offer children a chance to grow beautiful plants, but it also teaches them essential life skills and values. Scattered throughout the pages of this book is a multitude of benefits that gardening brings to the young ones. From encouraging responsibility and patience to developing a deep appreciation for the environment, gardening is a holistic learning experience that goes far beyond soil and seeds.

As parents and guardians, your active involvement and support in your children's gardening experience cannot be overstated. Participating alongside them creates a safe space for exploration, delightful discoveries, and shared memories. The garden becomes a canvas for quality time, where bonds are strengthened, and conversations flow freely.

Gardening is much more than the physical act of planting and tending to plants. It is an opportunity for deep personal growth. As you walk this journey with your children, you have the unique opportunity to motivate their curiosity by going on a quest for knowledge yourself. Become immersed in the fascinating world of plants, insects, and ecological concepts as a family. Let their questions take you on a path of exploration and research as you unravel the wonders of nature side by side. Encourage your children to express themselves through their garden projects. Let them choose their favorite plants, design their own small sections, and even make DIY garden decorations. By allowing their imagination to run free and granting them a sense of ownership, you give them the power to take pride in their creations and appreciate the beauty and significance hidden in each experience. And just like that, you will have sown the seeds of love for nature and reap the bountiful fruits of a patient, responsible, and creative child – and a shared gardening adventure.

Introduction Letter to Children

Hey there, kids!

Have you ever held a tiny seed in your hand? It's so small and simple. But within that humble shell lies the potential for greatness: the power to create life and beauty. With your tender care and protection, you will witness the miracle of that seed sprouting, stretching its green arms toward the sun, and transforming into the most precious plant. That is gardening. It is a front-row seat to the most captivating show on Earth.

But gardening is not just about witnessing miracles; it's about being a magician yourself. You'll learn the secrets of turning dry, lifeless soil into a fertile playground where plants live and bloom in peace. You'll discover the perfect balance of sun, water, and nutrients that will make your plants grow tall and proud. As you explore this delicate world as a gardener, nature will reward you with surprises at every turn: a hidden ladybug, a beautiful butterfly, or the refreshing smell of a blooming flower.

The garden is the most interesting classroom you'll ever walk into, where you'll soak up knowledge faster than the speed of a sprouting seed. Each plant you nurture will teach you things you never knew about biology, ecology, and how all living things are connected somehow. You'll become a detective, investigating the mysteries of pests and diseases, and a master problem-solver, finding the smartest ways to protect your green friends. Gardening is an adventure that promises laughter, surprises, and unforgettable moments. There are few experiences like the thrill of harvesting your own vegetables and biting into a juicy berry that you have grown with your own two hands. And when your friends come over, your garden will be the ultimate playground: a place of imagination and pure fun.

The pages of this book offer you all the inspiration, tips, and secrets you need. It's a portal to a world where plants whisper their wisdom, where you'll find answers to your burning questions, and where imagination takes root and grows alongside your plants. This book will be your trusted partner as you begin your life as a gardener. It will encourage you to dream big. It will guide you every step of the way, and before you know it, you will have gone from a curious beginner to a skilled gardener simply *because you can.*

Chapter One: Garden Basics

Garden basics are the building blocks of every garden. Just as a house needs a strong base to stand on, a garden needs a few important things to help it grow into something amazing. As a newbie gardener, you'll need all the basic ideas to start your garden, but gardening isn't just about facts and science. It's also about having fun and enjoying yourself!

A garden can bring so much joy to your life. Imagine watching a tiny seed sprout into a beautiful flower or a delicious vegetable you can eat. This experience connects you with nature. It teaches you to be patient and take care of things and gives you a peaceful place to relax. So, put on your gardening gloves and cool sun hat, and prepare to create the best garden in your neighborhood!

Finding Your Garden Location

When it comes to finding the perfect spot for your garden, there are a few things to keep in mind so that your plants come out strong and healthy.

First, sunlight. You need the sun to feel warm and full of energy, right? Plants need sunlight to make their food and grow big and strong. So, look for a place in your yard where the sun shines for at least six hours daily. That way, your plants will have plenty of sunshine to soak up.

Shade is nice on a hot day, but too much shade can make it hard for plants to get the sunlight they need. So, avoid spots under big, tall trees or buildings that block out a lot of sunlight. Plants like to bask in the warm sunbeams, too.

Look for a place in your yard that gets a lot of sun.
https://www.pexels.com/photo/green-grass-field-13975/

Next, check the soil. Think of soil as the cozy blanket that your plants snuggle into. You want the soil to be soft, crumbly, and easy for the plant roots to wiggle through. Take a look at the ground in your garden spot. If it's hard or rocky, you can make it better by adding some special stuff called compost or soil mix. It gives your plants a comfortable place to call home. Water is important too, just like it is for you. Plants need water to drink and stay hydrated. So, having a water source nearby, like a hose or a rain barrel, is a good idea. That way, you can easily give your plants a nice drink whenever they need it.

Finally, choose a garden spot that's easy for you to get to. You'll want to visit your garden as much as possible to take care of your plants, water them, and pick some vegetables or pretty flowers. So, pick a spot that's close to your house. That way, you can quickly hop, skip, and jump to your garden whenever you want.

How to Design Your Garden

Designing a garden makes you an artist, creating a beautiful masterpiece with plants and colors. Of course, there are a few things to think about, but the most important thing is to let your imagination run wild and be creative. Nonetheless, here are a few things to think about when designing the perfect garden:

- **Balance and Symmetry:** In your garden, you want to create balance by having tall plants or things on one side and shorter ones on the other. It's like having a big friend on one side of the seesaw and a smaller one on the other. This helps your garden look even and organized. Symmetry, however, means having things that look the same on both sides of your garden, like when you fold a piece of paper in half and both sides match. You can create symmetry by having two pretty flower beds or two pots with colorful flowers that look alike on both sides.

- **Size:** Next, consider size and proportion. See your garden as a big puzzle where all the pieces fit together just right. How much space do you have in your garden? Is it a big backyard or a small space? Your answer will help you decide how many plants and decorations you can fit in. Now, think about the size of the plants and objects you want to include. Some plants can grow really tall, like a giant sunflower, while others stay small and cute, like a tiny daisy. When you're drawing a picture, and you want everything to look right, you are applying the rules of *size and proportion*. You should do the same thing to your garden. For example, if you have a small garden, it might look funny if you put a huge tree in the middle, but if you have a big garden, a tall tree could be just right.

- **Color and Texture:** For color, you can choose flowers and plants in all different colors to make it look pretty. Imagine having red, yellow, blue, and purple flowers all together. It's an insane explosion of colors. You can even have flowers that change colors as the seasons go by, so your garden always looks new and exciting. Now, texture is all about how things feel when you touch them. Plants can have different textures in the same way that some toys are smooth and others are bumpy. Some leaves are soft and smooth, while others are rough or fuzzy. You can choose plants with different textures to make your garden fun to touch, not just fun to look at

You can choose different colored plants to make your garden look pretty.
https://www.pexels.com/photo/assorted-color-flowers-298246/

- **Decorations**: Feel free to add some pathways and cool decorations or toys. You can make paths that lead to different places in your garden, like secret hideouts or unique decorations. Use tiny stones, bricks, or even pebbles to make your paths. And don't forget the decorations, like a pretty statue, a shiny fountain, or a colorful bench. These things make your garden totally cool!

Fertilizing

Fertilizing is the act of giving food to plants so they can stay healthy and grow properly. Plants need nutrients like *nitrogen, phosphorus, and potassium* to survive and be happy. These nutrients help them make strong stems, beautiful leaves, and colorful flowers. But sometimes, the soil in a garden doesn't have enough of these nutrients, and that's when fertilizing comes in.

Fertilizers are *plant foods*. They are made with all the important nutrients that plants need. When you sprinkle or spread the fertilizer in the soil around the plants, they can suck it down into their roots. By adding fertilizers, you ensure that your plants have all the nutrients they need to be the best plants they can be.

Fertilizing also gives plants a shield against problems like diseases and pests. When plants get the right nutrients, they become strong and healthy. The same happens when you eat good food; you can fight germs better and not fall sick. Well-fed plants do it, too; they can protect themselves from nasty diseases and dangerous pests that can hurt them. So, by giving your plants the special plant food (fertilizer) they need, you're giving them the power to stay healthy and safe for as long as they live.

But remember, you have to be careful with fertilizers. Using too much can actually cause problems for your plants. It's like eating too much candy—it might taste good, but it's not good for your body. Too much fertilizer can hurt the roots of plants. So, you need to use the right amount and follow the instructions. You can ask an adult to help you with this. They can guide you on how much fertilizer to use and when. They can be your gardening buddy to make sure you're doing everything correctly.

Watering

Plants need water to quench their thirst and keep their stems happy, but you must be careful and water them correctly. When you water plants, it's best to pour the water at the base of the plant, near the roots. That's where the roots drink the water and send it to all parts of the plant. Instead of just splashing water on the leaves all the time, you'll be giving them a refreshing drink right where they need it the most. Every good gardener knows to avoid watering the leaves or flowers too much because it can make them wet for too long. Wet leaves and flowers can get sick and cause problems. You wouldn't want to stay wet for a long time, would you? You might catch a cold or get sick, too. For that reason, you should aim for the base of the plants as much as you can.

Plants need water to survive.
https://www.pexels.com/photo/person-watering-a-potted-plant-4503268/

Watering is important, but you must also find the right balance. You don't want to overwater or underwater your plants. Overwatering means giving them too much water, like pouring a whole bucket when they only need a little sip. Too much water can drown the roots and make the plant sick. This doesn't happen to just plants; if you drink too much water, you might feel sick and uncomfortable.

On the other hand, underwatering means not giving enough water to your plants, like when you're really thirsty and only get a tiny sip. If plants don't get enough water, they can become weak and wilted. They might not grow well, make pretty flowers, or produce good fruits.

So, how do you know when to water your plants? You can check the soil by sticking your finger about an inch deep into it. If it feels dry, it's time to water it, but you can wait a little longer if it feels wet. Each plant has different needs, so it's necessary to learn about the specific needs of the plants in your garden. Always remember watering plants is necessary, but you must do it right. Water at the base of the plants, avoid overwatering or underwatering – and check the soil so you know when your plants are thirsty!

Choosing Plants for Your Garden: All You Need to Know

1. **Space:** When choosing plants for your garden, consider how much space they need to grow. Some plants, like sunflowers, can grow really tall and need lots of room to spread their leaves. Other plants, like some herbs, stay small and can be grown in containers or small gardens. So, do your best to pick plants that fit nicely in your garden space.

2. **Care:** In the same way that we don't all have the same needs, plants have different needs, too. Some plants love to soak up the sun all day, while others prefer a bit of shade to keep them cool. Some plants need lots of water, while others are okay with less. For your sake and the sake of your garden, it's better to choose plants that match the conditions in your garden and are easy for you to take care of. That way, you and your plants have a relationship that you both enjoy.

3. **Fun Factor:** Your garden should definitely be super fun and exciting. You can choose plants that are unique and interesting. Look for flowers that attract butterflies with their bright colors and sweet smells. You can also find plants with cool shapes and textures, like fuzzy leaves or spiky flowers. All these plants will make your garden almost magical and the best one you've ever seen.

Chapter Two: Tools You'll Need

Garden tools can be the difference between a happy, healthy garden and a messy, untamed jungle. In gardening, tools are the instruments that help people take care of plants and make gardening easier and less like work. They save you time and energy by giving you faster ways to dig, prune, water, and maintain your garden. Without the right tools, tasks that should be fun can quickly become unending and frustrating. For example, using a shovel or trowel helps you dig holes faster than using just your hands. A watering can helps you water plants more evenly and without wasting water. Pruning shears make it quick and easy to trim plants so they stay healthy, and the other tools help you do different tasks in the garden without getting tired or messy. So, just like tools help you with different things at school or at home, gardening tools help you take care of plants and make gardening fun and easy.

Importance of Garden Tools

Garden tools can improve your gardening experience.
https://www.pexels.com/photo/person-wearing-green-gloves-holding-garden-tools-7782975/

Using the right garden tools will improve your garden and your gardening experience. Here's how:

1. **Get Things Done Faster**: Garden tools help you finish gardening tasks more quickly. They make digging, cutting, and taking out weeds easier and faster.
2. **Do Things Just Right**: Each garden tool is made for a specific job. They help you do things exactly the way you want. For example, pruning shears helps you cut branches neatly, and a trowel helps you make perfect little holes for planting.
3. **Get More Work Done**: When you use garden tools, you can do more work in less time. Tools like wheelbarrows, garden carts, and rakes help you move things like soil, leaves, and other stuff faster so you can finish your tasks quickly.
4. **Stay Safe and Protected**: Garden tools keep you safe while you work in the garden. Gloves, knee pads, and goggles protect you from thorns, sharp things, and dirt that can hurt you.
5. **Do Lots of Different Things**: Garden tools can do many different jobs. For example, a garden knife can dig, cut, and pull out weeds, while a garden fork helps loosen soil and move plants.
6. **Last a Long Time**: Good garden tools are strong and last a long time. If you care for them, they will keep working well for a while, so you won't have to buy new ones for years.
7. **Easy to Use**: Garden tools are made to be easy for everyone to use. They have comfortable handles and are not too heavy, so you can use them without getting tired or hurting yourself.
8. **Stay Organized**: Having garden tools helps you stay organized. You can keep them in one place; when you need them, they're ready to go. This way, you don't waste time looking for them.

Categories of Garden tools

- **Digging Tools**

Sometimes, you need to dig holes in the ground to plant seeds or move plants when gardening. There are special tools that can help you with this. One tool looks like a big scoop with a long handle. It's great for digging deep holes in the soil. Another tool is like a smaller scoop that fits in your hand. It's lighter and easier to use for digging smaller holes. There's also a tool that has a flat, square-shaped blade. It helps you dig and move soil when you need to make a trench or turn over the soil. And finally, there's a tool with pointy prongs. It's good for loosening the soil and breaking up clumps. These special tools make it easier for you to dig in the garden. Instead of your hands, use these tools to dig quickly and get the job done faster.

- **Cutting and Pruning Tools**

When caring for your plants, you will need to trim or cut away some parts to help them grow better. Cutting and pruning tools are simply scissors for plants. They help you remove extra branches or leaves that may be getting too big or are not healthy anymore. Just as you get haircuts to keep your hair healthy and neat, plants sometimes need a little trim, too!

- **Watering Tools**

Plants can't do without water because they need it to grow and stay healthy. You use tools to help give your plants the right amount of water. These tools help you gently pour water on the plants to ensure you give them the right amount, not too much or too little. They make it easier to water plants. You can water them evenly and ensure each plant gets the water it needs.

- **Planting Tools**

You use planting tools to plant new seeds or move plants to a different spot. Planting tools make putting the seeds or plants into the ground easier. They are the helpers that create little holes in the soil. You can then gently place the seeds or plants into these holes. Planting tools make planting so much easier; you have no idea! You can plant your favorite flowers, vegetables, or herbs without getting your hands all dirty.

- **Maintenance Tools**

Once in a while, your garden needs some tender, loving care, too. Maintenance tools keep your garden clean and healthy. One thing you will be doing as maintenance is removing the weeds. Weeds are unwanted plants that grow where you don't want them to. You can use these tools to pull them out of the ground so they don't take nutrients away from your plants.

Another thing you will be doing is tidying up your plants. Sometimes, they grow too big or have parts that are not healthy. You can use some tools to trim or cut away these extra parts. And remember to clean up fallen leaves or other messes in your garden. Use tools to gather the leaves and keep your garden neat. When you use maintenance tools, you take good care of your garden and ensure your plants have everything they need to look good and feel good. It is your way of showing your love and responsibility.

Basic Tools You'll Need

1. **Shovel:** A shovel is a tool with a long handle and a scoop-shaped blade at the end. It comes in many different sizes. It is used to dig holes in the ground. You can use a shovel to dig a hole for planting seeds or to transplant plants from one place to another.

2. **Watering Can:** A watering can is a special container with a spout and a handle. It is used to water plants. Fill the watering can with water and gently pour the water around the base of your plants. This helps them stay hydrated and healthy.

A watering can is used to water plants.
WayneRay, CC BY-SA 4.0 <https://creativecommons.org/licenses/by-sa/4.0>, via Wikimedia Commons: https://commons.wikimedia.org/wiki/File:Watering_can_WPC6.JPG

3. **Trowel:** A trowel is a small, handheld tool with a pointed blade. It is used to dig small holes when planting tiny flowers or herbs. Hold the handle of the trowel and push it into the soil to make a hole. Then, place your plant or seedling into the hole and cover it with soil.

4. **Gloves:** Gloves are protective covers for your hands. They keep your hands safe and clean while you work in the garden. Wear gloves to protect your hands from thorns, prickly plants, or dirt. They also prevent any scratches or cuts.
5. **Pruning Shears**: Pruning shears are scissors for plants. They trim or cut branches, leaves, or flowers from plants. When using pruning shears, be careful to only cut the parts of the plant that you need to. This will keep your plants looking good and encourage new growth.
6. **Rake:** A rake is a tool with a long handle and a row of teeth or prongs. It gathers leaves, grass, or other garden rubbish into piles. Hold the rake handle and slide it across the soil to gently gather the leaves or grass on the ground.

As easy as garden tools are to use, it is always safer to ask an adult for help and guidance. They can show you how to use the tools safely and teach you more about caring for plants.

Choosing the Best Tools for Your Age

When selecting tools for gardening, you should find ones that are just right for your age and size. Some tools are specially made in smaller sizes and designed for children like you. These tools are easier to hold and use because they are made with your needs in mind. Here are a few things to remember when you go shopping for tools:

1. **Size:** Look for tools that are smaller and lighter. They should fit well in your hands and be easy to hold. This way, you can use them comfortably without straining your muscles.
2. **Safety:** Safety is always important. Make sure the tools you choose have smooth edges and aren't too sharp. You want to avoid any accidents or cuts while working in the garden.
3. **Durability:** Find strong and durable tools; these will last a long time, and you can continue using them for many gardening adventures.
4. **Fun Designs:** Some gardening tools come in fun colors or with cool patterns. Choosing tools that you find visually interesting can make you excited to work in your garden.

Safety Rules

Nobody likes rules, but safety rules are not meant to hold you back or tell you what to do. They are there to keep you safe so that you are comfortable and have the best experience doing whatever you are doing. There are safety rules for everything, and that includes gardening and the use of garden tools. Here are the most important ones you should know:

- **Ask for Adult Supervision**: Always have an adult with you when using garden tools, at least at first. They can guide you and make sure you're using the tools safely.
- **Wear Safety Gear:** Wear gardening gloves to protect your hands from prickly plants and germs. Depending on the task, you might also need safety goggles to protect your eyes.
- **Use Tools for Their Intended Purpose**: Each tool has a specific job. Use the tools only for what they're meant to do. For example, don't use a trowel as a toy or a rake as a pretend sword. You might hurt yourself or, even worse, someone else.
- **Handle Tools with Care:** Treat your tools gently and with respect. Avoid swinging them around or playing rough games with them. Remember, they are not toys.
- **Watch Your Fingers**: Keep your fingers away from the sharp parts of the tools, like blades or prongs. Always pay attention to where they are while using the tools to avoid accidents.
- **Store Tools Properly:** When you have finished gardening for the day, put them away in a safe place. Store them where they won't be a tripping hazard or where younger children can't reach them.
- **Clean up After Yourself:** After using the tools, clean them and put them away neatly. This will keep the tools in good condition and make them last longer.
- **Be Aware of Your Surroundings:** Look around and make sure there are no obstacles or people nearby that you might accidentally hit with the tools. Give yourself plenty of space to work safely.

How to Clean and Care for Your Garden Tools

- **Step One: Gather Your Cleaning Supplies**: Get a bucket of warm, soapy water and a clean cloth or sponge.
- **Step Two: Remove Dirt and Debris**: Use a cloth or sponge to wipe off any dirt, mud, or plant residue from your tools. Make sure to clean both the blades and handles of your tools.
- **Step Three: Rinse with Water**: After removing the dirt, rinse your tools with clean water to wash away any remaining soap and dirt.
- **Step Four: Disinfect Your Tools**: To prevent the spread of diseases between plants, you should disinfect your tools. You can do this by using a solution of one part bleach to nine parts water. Get an adult for this. Dip a clean cloth or sponge into the solution and wipe down the blades and handles of your tools. Let them sit for a few minutes.
- **Step Five: Rinse and Dry**: After disinfecting, rinse your tools with clean water again to remove any leftover bleach. Then, use a dry cloth or towel to thoroughly dry your tools. Water can cause tools to rust, so drying them is important.
- **Step Six: Store in a Dry Place**: Once your tools are clean and dry, store them in a dry place. This prevents rust and keeps them in good condition for future use.
- **Step Seven: Clean Your Cleaning Supplies**: After cleaning your tools, remember to clean your bucket, cloth, or sponge. Rinse them thoroughly and let them dry before putting them away.

By cleaning and caring for your tools after each use, you're keeping them in good shape and preventing the spread of diseases that can harm your plants. It's a great way to take care of your tools and your garden at the same time.

Chapter Three: Fruits and Vegetables

You can enjoy fresh and tasty food all year round when you grow your own fruit and vegetables. You get to pick them when they are perfectly ripe and full of flavor, and that's way better than buying them from the store, where they might not be as fresh all the time. Eating fruit and vegetables is really good for your health. When you grow your own, you can choose to use natural ways to care for them. For example, you can use friendly bugs to eat the bad bugs or using compost instead of chemicals, keeping your harvest healthier and safer.

Growing your own food can also save you money. While you might need to spend a little bit of money to get started with seeds and tools, in the long run, it's much cheaper than buying fresh fruits and vegetables from the store. And the more you grow, the more you can save by storing or preserving them for later. When you grow your own food, you're also helping the environment. By not relying on food that has to travel long distances, you're doing your part to reduce pollution from transportation. You can also choose to use organic growing methods, which means no chemicals that can hurt the earth.

Gardening is a great way to get outside and stay active, but watching your plants grow and seeing them produce fruits is the icing on the cake. It's a project you have taken great care of, and it feels amazing when you see the results. It's something to be proud of and makes you feel really good about yourself. Growing your own food is also a chance to learn and discover new things. You get to learn how plants grow, how to care for them, and the bugs and animals that help them grow. It's your own mini-science experiment right in your backyard.

And finally, when you grow your own food, it can bring people together. You get to share what you grow with your friends, family, and neighbors. It's a great way to connect with others and have fun together. So, growing fruits and vegetables is not only exciting and rewarding, but it also helps you eat more healthily, save money, take care of the environment, learn new things, and make the best memories.

Soil Preparation

Preparing the soil is key to growing the sweetest and healthiest fruits and vegetables. First, understand that plants get their food from the soil. In the same way you need healthy food to grow strong as a human, plants need nutritious soil to grow big and tasty. So, soil preparation can translate to making the best meal for your plants.

Soil preparation is the key to growing the sweetest and healthiest fruits and vegetables.
https://www.pexels.com/photo/person-digging-on-soil-using-garden-shovel-1301856/

You start by clearing the area where you want to grow your plants. You remove any weeds or grass that might be there. This way, your plants have space to grow without any competition. Next, you need to loosen up the soil. You use tools like shovels or rakes to gently break up the soil. This helps the roots of the plants move around easily in the soil and reach the nutrients they need. After that, you add compost or natural fertilizers to the soil. Compost is made from fruit and vegetable scraps, leaves, and other organic materials. It's a special treat just for your soil. These natural fertilizers have lots of nutrients that plants love. They make the soil healthy and give your plants the energy they need to do their best.

Once you've added the compost, you need to mix it into the soil. Be gentle and take your time because you want the nutrients to spread evenly so that all your plants can get their fair share. Look at it like stirring a pot of soup to make sure all the ingredients blend together nicely. Now, your soil is ready for planting. You can put your seeds or tiny plants into the soil, cover them gently with some more soil, and give them a little drink of water. This helps them feel cozy and safe as they start to grow.

Why is all this soil preparation important? Well, you are creating a perfect home for your plants. You're giving them a good start in life and the best chance to produce the tastiest fruit and vegetables you've ever had. Gardening is a mission, and soil preparation is an important part of that mission. You owe it to your plants to get your hands dirty, mix in some compost, and make the soil fluffy and comfortable for them.

Soil Testing and Amending

Soil testing is a check-up for the soil. It helps you understand what the soil is like and what extra things it might need to make your plants happy. To do a soil test, you take a small soil sample and send it to a special lab. The scientists in the lab will test the soil to see what nutrients it has and if anything is missing. You can also buy soil testing kits. Once you get the soil test results, you can know if your soil needs any adjustments. Sometimes, the soil might have less nutrients than your plants need; if that is the case, you can amend it.

Amending means adding things to the soil to make it better. You can add compost, manure, or organic fertilizers to prepare the soil for planting. Adding compost to your garden gives the plants more nutrients to eat and helps the soil hold onto water like a sponge. Manure might sound a little funny, but it's actually poop from animals, particularly cows, chickens, or horses. But don't worry; it's clean and safe for your plants. It contains the necessary things to grow, like nitrogen, phosphorus, and potassium. Think vitamin shake, but ONLY for plants.

Planting: The Process

Planting seeds, seedlings, or young plants is an exciting part of growing fruits and vegetables. You'll need some tips to help you with this:

- **Start by Preparing the Soil:** Clear the area where you want to plant your seeds or seedlings. Remove any weeds or grass to give your plants space to grow.
- **Dig a Hole:** Use a small shovel or your hands to dig a hole in the soil. The hole should be deep enough for the roots of your plants to fit comfortably.
- **Planting Seeds:** If you're planting seeds, follow the instructions on the seed packet. Some seeds need to be planted deeper, while others should be closer to the surface. Drop the seeds into the hole and cover them with a thin layer of soil. Gently pat the soil down to make sure the seeds are snug and secure.
- **Planting Seedlings or Young Plants:** If you're planting seedlings or young plants, gently remove them from their pots or containers. Place the root ball (the clump of soil around the roots) into the hole you have dug, and make sure the plant stands up straight. Then, cover the roots with soil, gently patting it down around the base of the plant.
- **Proper Planting Depth:** Seeds or seedlings do better if planted correctly. Too deep, and they might struggle to reach the surface. Too shallow, and they may not get enough support. The seed packet or instructions that come with seedlings usually tell you how deep to plant them. Follow those guidelines to make sure you're doing it right.
- **Spacing Your Plants:** Each plant needs space to spread its roots. If plants are too close together, they'll start fighting for sunlight, water, and food. The seed packet or instructions should inform you of how much space each plant needs. Leave enough room between plants so that they have space to grow without crowding each other or fighting all the time.
- **Water Your Plants:** After planting, give your seeds, seedlings, or young plants a nice drink of water. This helps them settle into their new home and gives them the moisture they need to start their lives.

Proper Watering Practices

- Give your plants a drink about one knuckle deep when the soil feels dry.
- Pour the water close to the bottom of the plant, where the roots are.
- Use a watering can with a spout or a gentle hose to water your plants.
- Water your plants in the morning or evening when it's not too hot outside.
- Don't give your plants too much water. Just make the soil feel damp, like a sponge wrung out, but not soaking wet like a puddle.
- Watch out for signs that your plants are thirsty, for example, leaves that look droopy or soil that feels really dry.
- If you have delicate plants, be extra careful when you water them. Use a mist or spray bottle to moisten the soil.
- Before you water your plants, check the weather forecast. If rain is on the way, you might not need to water them as much. You can adjust how often you water based on what the weather is doing.

Fruits

Apples

- **Edible Parts**: Apples have a tasty and crunchy part that you can eat. It's the juicy part around the core in the middle.
- **Seeds:** Apples have tiny seeds inside the middle part, the core.
- **Proper Care:** To grow apple trees, find a sunny spot with soil that drains water well. Give them enough water, and trim them regularly.

Things to Remember

1. Apple trees need help from other apple trees to make lots of fruits. So, it's a good idea to plant two different kinds of apple trees close to each other.
2. Sometimes, apple trees grow too many apples, so it's better to take some fruit off the tree. That way, the ones that are left will

be bigger and sweeter.

Raspberries
- **Edible Parts:** The juicy berries that grow on prickly branches.
- **Seeds:** Raspberries have tiny seeds hiding inside the berry.
- **Proper Care:** Raspberry plants prefer to be placed somewhere sunny in soil that lets water drain away. Help the branches climb by giving them something to hold onto, and make sure to give them water regularly.

Things to Remember
1. Trim the old branches of raspberry plants to make room for new ones to grow.
2. Pick raspberries when they are fully ripe and come easily off the plant.

Blueberry

Blueberries are small and round.
Photo by Joanna Kosinska on Unsplash <u>https://unsplash.com/photos/blueberries-on-white-ceramic-container-4qujjbj3srs</u>

- **Edible Parts:** The small, round berries that taste sweet and tangy.
- **Seeds:** Inside the berry, you can find tiny seeds.
- **Proper Care:** For blueberry plants, find a place with slightly acidic soil that lets water flow away. They like to be in the sun, but some shade is okay, too. Make sure to give them water regularly so the soil stays damp.

Things to Remember
1. Blueberries like acidic soil, so you can add peat moss or pine needles to make the soil more acidic.
2. During the season when the plants aren't growing much, trim off the old branches to make room for new ones to grow.

Watermelon
- **Edible Parts:** The juicy and sweet flesh inside their big, green outer shell.
- **Seeds:** Watermelons have a lot of seeds inside.
- **Proper Care:** Watermelon plants like a lot of sun and soil that doesn't soak up too much water. Give them lots of water, though, especially when it's hot and dry.

Things to Remember
1. Watermelon plants like to spread out, so make sure they have lots of space to grow.
2. Pick the watermelon when the bottom part changes from light green to creamy yellow.

Tomato
- **Edible Parts:** The round, juicy parts that come in red or yellow colors.
- **Seeds:** Inside the tomato, you can find lots of tiny seeds.
- **Proper Care:** Tomato plants love the sun and light soil with good drainage. Give them water regularly so the soil is always a little wet.

Things to Remember
1. Tomato plants are naturally climbing plants, so they need something to lean on and support them, like sticks or cages, to stay upright as they grow.
2. Take away extra branches called suckers to help the plant use its energy for making fruits.

Vegetables

Carrot
- **Edible Parts:** Carrots have long, crunchy orange roots that you can eat.

- **Seeds:** To grow carrots, you will need to buy carrot seeds.
- **Proper Care:** When you want to grow carrot plants, find loose and sandy soil. Water them regularly so the soil stays damp.

Things to Remember
1. To help your carrots, remove some of the seedlings to give each carrot enough space.
2. Putting a layer of mulch around the plants can keep the soil cool and save water.

Pumpkin

Pumpkin.

Photo by Marius Ciocirlan on Unsplash https://unsplash.com/photos/orange-pumpkins-on-gray-field-near-green-grassland-at-daytime-selective-focus-photography-T9pdHqCsyoQ

- **Edible Parts:** The sweet, orange flesh inside the tough outer shell.
- **Seeds:** Inside the pumpkin, you can find big seeds.
- **Proper Care:** Pumpkins need lots of space to spread out, so your garden needs to be big enough. Remember to water them really well.

Things to Remember
1. Pumpkin plants like to have lots of room, so make sure they have plenty of space to grow big.
2. Pick the pumpkins when fully ripe and the outside is hard.

Build a Specialty Garden

A specialty garden is a rare kind of garden that focuses on growing specific types of plants or creating a unique theme. It's a garden that is all about one particular thing that you really like. Take a look at some pretty good examples:

1. **Butterfly Garden:** A butterfly garden is designed to attract beautiful butterflies. You can plant colorful flowers that butterflies love, like daisies and milkweed. By creating a butterfly garden, you can watch them flutter around and land on the flowers, looking for food.

2. **Fairy Garden:** A fairy garden is a magical garden full of tiny decorations and plants. You will be creating a mini-world for fairies to visit by using small houses, tiny furniture, and even tiny fairy figurines. Planting small flowers, like forget-me-nots and pansies, adds to the enchantment. Who knows? You might find a fairy hiding in your garden one day.

3. **Pizza Garden:** A pizza garden has to be the best idea ever thought of. Here, you can grow ingredients to make as many pizzas as you want. You can plant tomato plants for the sauce, basil for the herbs, bell peppers for toppings, and even onions. It's a garden full of the delicious things you need to make your very own homemade pizzas.

Chapter Four: Herbs and Flowers

Herbs are the cool cousins of the plant world. They are small but mighty, with leaves you can use to make your food taste delicious. Pizza with oregano sprinkled on top is a great example. Most herbs also have powers you probably didn't know about. Some herbs, like chamomile, can help you relax and have a good night's sleep. Others, like peppermint, can make your tummy feel better when it is upset. Flowers, on the other hand, are nature's artists. They paint the world with their breathtaking beauty. From the happy faces of daisies to the delicate petals of roses, flowers come in all shapes, sizes, and colors. They're a living example of nature's artistry.

The Value of Growing Herbs and Flowers in Your Garden

1. **Colors and Beauty:** When you grow herbs and flowers, you get to have all sorts of colors in your garden. It could be filled with bright red, jolly yellow, and pretty purple flowers.
2. **Fragrances and Scents:** Have you ever smelled a flower and automatically felt better? Flowers have different scents; some are fresh or even spicy. Some flowers smell deliciously sweet, while others are more calming. Growing flowers in your garden means you get to enjoy all of these scents and make your garden smell fantastic for anyone who decides to visit.

3. **Helping Bees and Butterflies:** Bees and butterflies are more important to the world than you think, and they need all the help they can get for their super-important mission. They help plants by moving pollen from one flower to another, and this helps new plants grow and make more food. By growing herbs and flowers in your garden, you'll feed these pollinators with as much nectar as needed. They'll come buzzing and flying around, making your garden their favorite hangout spot.
4. **Tasty Flavors:** Herbs are also flavor boosters for your food. Have you ever tried fresh basil in your pasta sauce or sprinkling mint leaves in your lemonade? Growing herbs in your garden means you can add all of these flavors and more to your meals. You'll have a mini herb store right outside.
5. **Sharing and Gifting:** You get to pick a bunch of beautiful flowers from your garden and give them to someone special. You can make someone's day brighter with a very simple gift.

Useful Herbs and Flowers to Grow in Your Garden

Whether you have a green thumb or are just starting your first garden, these herbs and flowers have been specifically designed for children's gardens. Here, you have different herbs and flowers that are easy to care for, very pretty to look at, and lovely to smell. Take a look:

Herbs for Children's Gardens

Basil (Ocimum basilicum)

Basil.
Photo by Yakov Leonov on Unsplash https://unsplash.com/photos/green-leaves-in-macro-lens-0wWYos3ZGqU

- **Description**: Basil is a unique herb with leaves that smell and taste amazing. It comes in different types, like sweet basil, lemon basil, and purple basil.
- **Planting:** Plant basil in soil that gets lots of sunlight. Make sure the soil is not too wet, and there is some space between each plant.
- **Watering**: Give basil enough water to keep the soil moist but not soggy. Don't forget to water it regularly, especially on hot days.
- **Tip:** If you want more basil leaves for cooking, pinch off the little flowers that grow on top.

Mint (Mentha spp.)

- **Description**: Mint is a refreshing herb that smells just like a cool breeze. There are different kinds, but the most popular are peppermint and spearmint.
- **Planting:** Plant mint in a pot or a separate part of the garden because it spreads quickly. It likes some shade, as it doesn't like getting too hot.
- **Watering**: Keep the soil damp but not soaked. Mint likes to drink water regularly, especially in hot weather.
- **Tip:** To make sure the mint stays bushy and doesn't get too tall, trim the stems regularly.

Chives (Allium schoenoprasum)

- **Description**: Chives look like spring onions, but they are tinier with pretty purple flowers. They taste delicious, too.
- **Planting:** Put chives in areas with some sunlight, but not too much. Leave space between each plant.
- **Watering:** Chives need regular drinks of water, but let the soil dry out a bit between watering.
- **Tip:** Snip the long leaves from the bottom to help new leaves grow. It's also a good idea to remove the flowers before they bloom.

Dill (Anethum graveolens)

- **Description**: Dill has feathery leaves and bright yellow flowers that butterflies love.

- **Planting:** Plant dill in a place that gets lots of sun. Leave some space between each plant.
- **Watering:** Give dill enough water so the soil stays moist but not too wet.
- **Tip:** Harvest the leaves and seeds often to keep the plant healthy and prevent it from flowering too quickly.

Lemon Balm (Melissa officinalis)
- **Description:** Lemon balm has cute little white flowers and leaves that smell like lemons.
- **Planting:** Put lemon balm in a slightly sunny spot. Leave a bit of space between each plant.
- **Watering:** Keep the soil moist by watering regularly.
- **Tip:** Trim the plant often, especially the top, to make it grow fuller and not too tall.

Flowers for Children's Gardens

Marigold (Tagetes spp.)

Marigolds.
Photo by Julia Kwiek on Unsplash https://unsplash.com/photos/orange-flowers-with-green-leaves-2j8X-RpB1sM

- **Description:** Marigolds have flowers in bright colors like yellow, orange, and red. They look just like tiny suns.
- **Planting:** Place marigolds in an area that gets lots of sun. Give each plant enough space to grow.

- **Watering:** Water marigolds when the soil feels dry, and don't forget to give them a drink regularly.
- **Tip:** If you remove the flowers that have finished blooming, you'll make room for new ones to grow.

Sunflower (Helianthus annuus)
- **Description:** Sunflowers are tall plants with big, happy flowers that follow the sun as it moves across the sky.
- **Planting:** Plant sunflower seeds directly in soil that gets lots of sun. Give each plant some space to grow because they can get massive.
- **Watering:** Water sunflowers when the soil feels dry. They like a good drink regularly.
- **Tip:** Use sticks or supports to help the tall sunflowers stand up straight.

Nasturtium (Tropaeolum spp.)
- **Description:** Nasturtiums have flowers in beautiful colors like red, orange, and yellow. They also taste a little spicy.
- **Planting:** Plant nasturtiums under a bit of sun, but not too much. Give each plant some space to spread out.
- **Watering:** Water nasturtiums when the soil feels dry. They like to stay a bit dry between watering.
- **Tip:** If you remove the flowers that have gone over, more new flowers will keep growing.

Zinnia (Zinnia spp.)
- **Description:** Zinnias come in many colors, like pink, purple, red, and orange.
- **Planting:** Plant zinnias where they'll get lots of sun. Each plant needs its own space to grow properly.
- **Watering:** Water zinnias when the soil feels dry. They like regular drinks of water.
- **Tip:** If you remove the flowers that have finished blooming, new ones will keep popping up.

Pansy (Viola spp.)

Pansy.
https://unsplash.com/photos/purple-and-yellow-flower-in-tilt-shift-lens-Md_rDAJxRLM?utm_content=creditShareLink&utm_medium=referral&utm_source=unsplash

- **Description:** Pansies have flowers with pretty faces in colors like purple, yellow, blue, and white. They look like they're smiling at you.
- **Planting:** Pansies like sunny spots and a bit of shade sometimes. They also need space to grow.
- **Watering:** Water pansies when the soil feels dry. They like to stay a little dry between watering.
- **Tip:** Pinch off the tall parts of the plant to help it grow bushier. And if you remove the flowers that are done, more flowers will keep blooming.

Using Herbs in the Kitchen

Herbs add flavor and aroma to dishes, take you on a ride through the culinary world, and let you get creative in the kitchen. Here are some herbs and recipes you can experiment with:

- **Basil:** Basil has a sweet and slightly peppery flavor. It's perfect for adding to salads, pasta dishes, and sandwiches. You can try making caprese skewers by threading cherry tomatoes, small mozzarella balls, and fresh basil leaves onto skewers. Drizzle with a little olive oil and balsamic glaze for a tasty and colorful snack.

- **Mint:** Mint has a refreshing and cool taste. You can add it to your drinks, salads, and desserts. A fun idea is to make minty lemonade by squeezing fresh lemon juice, adding some chopped mint leaves, and sweetening it with a bit of honey or sugar. Mix it all together with water and ice, and it's ready to go.
- **Chives:** Chives have a mild onion flavor. They can be sprinkled on soups, baked potatoes, and scrambled eggs. You can make cheesy chive omelets by whisking eggs, adding chopped chives, grated cheese, and a pinch of salt. Cook the mixture in a pan until it sets, and enjoy a delicious and protein-packed breakfast.
- **Dill:** Dill has a unique flavor that is often linked to pickles. It pairs well with fish, potatoes, and salads. Try preparing a creamy dill dip by mixing Greek yogurt, chopped dill, garlic powder, and a squeeze of lemon juice. Serve it with carrot sticks, cucumber slices, or whole-grain crackers for something healthy and tasty.
- **Rosemary:** Rosemary has a strong and aromatic flavor. It's great for seasoning roasted vegetables, chicken, and potatoes. You can try rosemary roasted potatoes by tossing diced potatoes with olive oil, minced rosemary leaves, salt, and pepper. Bake in the oven until crispy and golden brown.

Design Ideas for Your Herb and Flower Garden

1. **Rainbow Meadow**

   Create a rainbow in your garden by planting flowers of different colors in rows or clusters. Start with red flowers like roses or tulips, then move on to orange marigolds, yellow sunflowers, green ferns, blue pansies, indigo petunias, and finally, purple lavender.

2. **Colorful Containers**

   If you are using pots or containers, paint them in bright, fun colors and shades of red, yellow, or even blue. Then, plant different flowers in each container, matching the colors of the pots. For example, you could plant red geraniums in the red pot, yellow marigolds in the yellow pot, and blue lobelia in the blue pot.

3. **Pollinator Paradise**

    Design a garden that attracts pollinators like bees and butterflies. Choose flowers that are both colorful and rich in nectar, such as bee balm, coneflowers, and sunflowers. You can also add some herbs like lavender, mint, or basil, which pollinators love, too.

4. **Sensory Sensation**

    Try building a garden that engages all your senses. Choose flowers with different textures; some common ones are woolly lamb's ear or velvety pansies. Then include plants with interesting smells, maybe scented geraniums or chocolate-scented cosmos. You can even add wind chimes or a small water feature for soothing sounds.

Chapter Five: Harvest Time

It's time to celebrate all the hard work you've put into your garden and get ready to harvest your hard-earned rewards. Harvesting means picking the fruit, vegetables, and herbs grown in your garden. It's an exciting and rewarding moment in gardening. You've watered, nurtured, and watched your plants grow, and now it's time to enjoy the fruits of your labor. It's a special moment when you see your hard work transform into something you can taste, smell, and enjoy.

Harvesting allows you to see the hard work you've put into your garden.
https://www.pexels.com/photo/vegetables-harvest-fresh-basket-175414/

Knowing When to Harvest

It's easy to tell when fruit, vegetables, and herbs are ready to be harvested if you know what to look for. Here are some clues:

- **Color:** Fruit and vegetables that are ripe have obvious, bright colors. For example, strawberries turn bright red when they're ready to be picked, and carrots become a rich orange color. So, keep an eye out for colors that pop.
- **Size Matters:** As fruit and vegetables grow, they get bigger and reach a certain size when they're just right. For instance, zucchinis should be about 6-8 inches long before being picked. So, compare the size of your plants to pictures or samples to see if they're ready.
- **Ripeness:** Ripeness is all about taste and texture. Some fruits and vegetables become sweeter and juicier as they ripen. For example, when watermelons are ready, they sound hollow when you tap them and have a sweet aroma. Tomatoes are ripe when firm but slightly soft when gently squeezed. And herbs are at their best when they have a strong scent. Trust your senses to tell you if something is ripe and ready to go into your basket.

Of course, not everything in the garden ripens at the same time. Some plants take longer, while others are ready sooner. So, check your plants regularly to catch them at their tastiest moments.

How to Harvest Different Fruits, Vegetables, and Herbs

- **Cutting Crops**

When it's time to harvest different crops from the garden, you can use a few methods. You use scissors or garden snips to carefully cut crops like lettuce. Hold the stem of the lettuce gently and snip it close to the base. Remember to cut only what you need so the plant can keep growing and producing more.

- **Picking Fruits and Vegetable**

To pick strawberries, just hold them gently and give them a tug.
https://commons.wikimedia.org/wiki/File:Wild_strawberries_ARS.jpg

For fruit and vegetables like tomatoes, strawberries, or cucumbers, you use your hands to pick them. Hold the fruit or vegetable gently and give it a little twist or tug. If it comes off the plant easily, it's ready to be harvested.

- **Gently Pulling**

Some crops, like carrots or radishes, are pulled straight from the ground. Hold the green leaves firmly near the base and give them a gentle pull. The root vegetables will come out with a satisfying "pop." Just be careful not to pull too hard, or the leaves might come off without the root.

- **Snipping Herbs**

Herbs like basil, mint, or parsley have their own special techniques. The best time to harvest herbs is in the morning after the dew has dried but before it gets too hot. This is when the herbs have the most flavor. To harvest, use scissors or garden snips to snip off the leaves or stems just above a set of leaves. This way, the plant can grow and produce more leaves.

If you have more herbs than you can use right away, you can preserve them for later. One way is by drying them. Gather a bunch of herb stems, tie them together with string, and hang them upside down in a cool, dry place. Once dry and crisp, crumble the leaves into a jar for future use. Another option is freezing herbs. Chop them up, place them in ice cube trays, and fill each cube with water. Pop them in the freezer, and when you need herbs for a recipe, grab a herb cube and toss it in.

Taking Care of Your Harvest

Caring for your harvest keeps it fresh and delicious. When you harvest anything, you want to avoid bruising or damaging your precious goodies to keep them fresh for longer. Fruits and vegetables can get bruised or squished if you're not careful, making them go bad faster. But when you treat them gently, they stay nice and tasty.

Besides, you've put so much effort into growing your garden, and you want to enjoy the fruits (and vegetables) of your labor. By handling them carefully, you show respect for all your hard work. Plus, eating something that looks as good as it tastes is more fun. Bring a basket or a container when you go out to harvest. You can gently place your fruit, vegetables, and herbs inside, keeping them safe and snug. Baskets or containers protect your produce and prevent them from getting squished or bumped as you move around the garden.

Harvest Recipes

You can create delicious meals using the ingredients you've grown. Here are some simple and easy recipes that you can try at home:

- **Garden Veggie Pizza**

For this recipe, you'll need a pizza crust, tomato sauce, and as many fresh vegetables as you can get from your garden. Start by spreading the tomato sauce on the crust. Then, get creative and add your favorite garden produce, like tomatoes, bell peppers, onions, and even some basil leaves. Top it off with a sprinkle of cheese, and ask a grown-up to help you bake it until the cheese is nice and bubbly.

- **Fresh Strawberry Parfait**

This is the easiest recipe for your garden-grown strawberries. Grab a clear glass or a fancy cup and layer it with fresh strawberries, a dollop of yogurt, and a sprinkle of granola or crushed cookies. Repeat the layers until your cup is full, and you're good to go.

- **Garden Veggie Wraps**

For these tasty wraps, you'll need large lettuce leaves (like romaine or butter lettuce) from your garden, sliced cucumbers, shredded carrots, and any other veggies you love. Spread some creamy hummus or cream cheese on the lettuce leaf, then pile on the veggies. Roll it up like a burrito, and you've got a garden-fresh wrap ready to eat.

- **Cheesy Zucchini Bites**

Zucchinis are a fantastic garden vegetable to use in this recipe. Grate a zucchini and squeeze out any excess moisture. Mix it with breadcrumbs, grated cheese, an egg (with the help of a grown-up), and some seasonings like salt and pepper. Shape the mixture into little patties and cook them in a pan until golden brown on both sides.

- **Stuffed Bell Peppers**

Bell peppers are colorful and make a great container for stuffing. Cut the tops off the peppers and remove the seeds. Mix cooked rice, diced tomatoes, corn kernels, cooked ground meat (like beef or turkey), and some shredded cheese in a bowl. Spoon the mixture into the hollowed-out bell peppers. Place them on a baking sheet and get a grown-up to bake them in the oven until the peppers are tender and the filling is hot and bubbly.

Cooking is a way to express your creativity, so feel free to switch up these recipes to suit your taste and the ingredients you have on hand. Experimenting with the flavors in your garden is a wonderful way to appreciate the magic of growing your own food, so have fun in the kitchen and enjoy the rewards of your garden harvest.

Chapter Six: Garden Friends and Pests

This chapter is for the tiny creatures that play a role of some kind in all the green spaces. You'll learn about the helpful and not-so-friendly ones and how they can affect your garden. Every farm or garden has a whole community of insects and animals buzzing around or scurrying about. Some of them are your garden champions, like bees and ladybugs, who work hard to pollinate flowers and eat harmful pests that can damage your plants. The others are critters that cause trouble. These are the pests, like aphids or slugs, that munch on your plants and make them sick. They're not the best guests at your garden party – but don't worry, you can manage them.

By learning about the different types of insects and animals in your garden, you can become an expert detective who knows how to identify them, understand their behaviors, and determine whether they're beneficial or harmful. That way, you can create a garden where the good bugs are welcome and the pests are bounced at the door.

Beneficial Insects

Here are some beneficial insects and pollinators you can find in gardens, along with tips on how to attract them:

- **Bees**

Bees are fantastic pollinators.
https://unsplash.com/photos/honeybee-perching-on-yellow-flower-yxXpjF-RrnA?utm_content=creditShareLink&utm_medium=referral&utm_source=unsplash

Pollinators are like the superheroes of the plant world! Bees are a famous example, but butterflies, hummingbirds, and even some bats are pollinators!

Here's what they do: when they go from flower to flower to drink nectar, which is a sweet liquid that flowers make, they get pollen on their bodies. Pollen is a yellow, powdery substance that plants need to make seeds.

When a pollinator visits another flower, the pollen rubs off onto that flower. This helps the flower create seeds that can grow into new plants. It's like the pollinators are helping the flowers send messages to each other so they can make more flowers! Thanks to pollinators, we have lots of fruits and vegetables to eat, and so do many animals in the wild. So, next time you see a bee buzzing around flowers, remember it's doing a super important job!

So, be sure to plant various flowering plants with different shapes and colors to attract bees to your garden. Bees love flowers like sunflowers, lavender, and wildflowers. Also, keep a shallow water source nearby, like a small dish with stones for them to land on, so they can stay hydrated while they fly around doing their thing.

- **Ladybugs**

Ladybugs eat harmful pests.
https://unsplash.com/photos/macro-photography-of-orange-and-black-bug-perching-on-plant-906sxg0humM?utm_content=creditShareLink&utm_medium=referral&utm_source=unsplash

Ladybugs are adorable and helpful insects that eat harmful pests like aphids. To attract ladybugs, grow plants like dill, fennel, and marigold. You can also create a ladybug house by tying together a few small sticks or bamboo pieces and placing them in a sheltered spot. Ladybugs will move in as soon as they find it and help keep your garden pest-free.

- **Butterflies**

Butterflies are not only beautiful but also important pollinators. Plant nectar-rich flowers such as milkweed, zinnias, and lantanas to attract butterflies. Create a butterfly puddling station by filling a shallow dish with sand and keeping it moist. Butterflies love to sip water and extract minerals from the damp sand.

- **Ground Beetles**

Ground beetles feast on pests.
Photo by Ingo Doerrie on Unsplash <https://unsplash.com/photos/close-up-photography-of-beetle-btmrHN8V3B0>

Ground beetles are nighttime hunters that feast on slugs, snails, and other pests. To attract ground beetles, prepare a tiny house for them with mulch or leaf piles. They also like plants with small flowers, such as daisies and asters. By keeping your garden diverse and setting up hiding spots, you'll let these beetles know they are welcome to stay and help.

- **Lacewings**

Lacewings are delicate insects that consume aphids, mealybugs, and other soft-bodied pests. Plant pollen and nectar-rich flowers such as dandelions, cosmos, and coreopsis to attract lacewings. Or you can buy lacewing eggs or larvae from garden supply stores and release them to grow and multiply in your garden.

- **Hoverflies**

Hoverflies, also known as flower flies, are excellent pollinators and aphid-eaters. To attract hoverflies, include plants like yarrow, daisies, and calendula in your garden. They love flowers with flat tops where they can land easily. Avoid using chemical pesticides because hoverflies are sensitive to them and may get sick.

Harmful Pests

Here are some common garden pests and tips on how to manage them:

- **Aphids**

Aphids are small, sap-sucking insects that can damage your plants. To deal with aphids, encourage natural predators like ladybugs and lacewings by planting flowers that attract them, such as daisies and fennel. You can also spray a mixture of water and mild dish soap onto affected plants to chase away aphids.

- **Whiteflies**

Whiteflies feed on plant sap.
xpda, CC BY-SA 4.0 <https://creativecommons.org/licenses/by-sa/4.0>, via Wikimedia Commons: https://commons.wikimedia.org/wiki/File:Aleyrodidae_P1560540a.jpg

Whiteflies are tiny, flying insects that feed on plant sap and can cause leaf yellowing and wilting. To control whiteflies, bring in natural enemies like parasitic wasps and predatory beetles into your garden. Yellow sticky traps placed near infested plants can also help catch adult whiteflies.

- **Slugs and Snails**

Slugs and snails are nighttime pests that can chew holes in leaves and stems. To control them, physical barriers like copper tape or *diatomaceous earth* should be put up around vulnerable plants. Diatomaceous earth is a super cool, powdery substance that comes from the fossilized remains of tiny, aquatic creatures called diatoms. Think of diatoms as really small algae that have a hard shell. Over millions of years, these shells piled up on the bottom of oceans or lakes and turned into a kind of rock. When this rock is ground up, it turns into a fine, white powder –that's diatomaceous earth!

It's sort of like magic dust for gardeners because it helps keep bugs away from plants without using chemicals. It works by sticking to the bugs that crawl over it, and since it's sharp on a microscopic level, it scratches the bugs and makes them lose water and dry out. But don't worry, it's safe for people and pets when used properly!

You can also set up slug traps filled with beer or yeast solution to attract and drown them. Handpicking them off plants in the evening or early morning and disposing of them can also be effective.

How to Identify and Manage Pests

These are a few methods you can try to help you identify and manage pests in your garden.

Physical Control

1. Look closely at your plants and check for any signs of pests, like holes in leaves or chewed stems.
2. If you spot pests, you can physically remove them by gently picking them off with your hands or using tweezers.
3. For larger pests like slugs or snails, you can set up barriers around the plants using materials like crushed eggshells or diatomaceous earth. These two things create a rough surface that the pests don't like to crawl over.
4. You can also set up traps, like shallow dishes filled with beer or yeast solution, to attract and catch pests like slugs. Remember to check the traps regularly and toss any trapped pests you find.

Safety Guidelines

- Always wash your hands thoroughly after handling pests.
- If you're not really sure how to handle a particular pest, ask an adult for help.

Biological Control

1. Learn about the good insects that can help control pests in your garden, such as ladybugs or praying mantises.

2. Create a welcoming environment for these insects by planting flowers that attract them, like daisies or marigolds.
3. You can also buy or build special houses or shelters designed for them.
4. Once the beneficial insects move in, they naturally eat the pests and help keep their numbers in check.

Safety Guidelines
- Be gentle and careful when handling beneficial insects to avoid harming them.
- Avoid chemical pesticides, as they can harm beneficial insects and your garden ecosystem.

Cultural Control
1. Practice good garden hygiene by regularly removing fallen leaves, weeds, and dirt. Pests often hide in these areas.
2. Rotate your crops each year. This means planting different types of plants in different spots. It prevents pests from building up in the soil and attacking the same plants year after year.
3. Water your plants properly. Some pests like to hang out on wet leaves, so it's better to water your plants at the base and avoid overwatering.

Safety Guidelines
- Use gloves to protect your hands from sharp objects or thorns when cleaning up garden debris.

Non-Chemical, Holistic Control Methods

1. Make your own natural pest repellents. For example, you can mix water and mild liquid soap to create a spray that scares off pests like aphids.
2. Plant companion plants that repel pests. Some plants, like marigolds or basil, have natural properties that pests don't like.
3. Create a healthy garden ecosystem by attracting birds, butterflies, and other beneficial wildlife. They can help control pests naturally.

Safety Guidelines
- Follow the instructions and measurements carefully when making homemade pest repellents.

- Ask an adult for help when handling or mixing ingredients.
- Observe and check on your garden regularly because pest problems can arise at any time.

Chapter Seven: Tips and Troubleshooting

By now, you probably agree that gardening is a neat way to get your own plants, whether beautiful flowers or juicy vegetables. But this method is not foolproof; sometimes, plants have problems, too. Don't worry, though, because most of these problems can be fixed with some know-how and simple actions. In this chapter, you will look at some common issues that gardeners usually face, how to recognize these problems, and what to do about them. This should get you started:

Pests

- **Recognize:** Look for tiny insects or holes in the leaves.
- **Action:** Pick off pests by hand or use natural sprays like soapy water.

Weeds

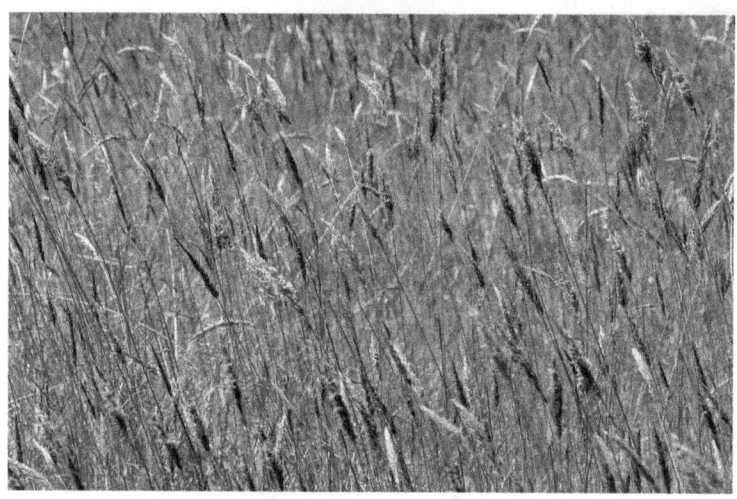

Weeds can harm your plants.
Sharon Mollerus, CC BY 2.0 <https://creativecommons.org/licenses/by/2.0>, via Wikimedia Commons: https://commons.wikimedia.org/wiki/File:Field_of_Weeds_(2636333676).jpg

- **Recognize:** Notice unwanted plants growing among your flowers or vegetables.
- **Action**: Pull out weeds by hand, *making sure to get the roots.*

Diseases

- **Recognize:** Observe spots, discoloration, or wilting on plants.
- **Action:** Remove infected leaves or plants, and use organic fungicides if it looks too bad.

Overwatering

- **Recognize:** Watch for waterlogged soil or yellowing, droopy leaves.
- **Action:** Reduce watering and let the soil dry out between watering.

Underwatering

- **Recognize:** Look for dry, crispy leaves or wilted plants.
- **Action:** Water plants thoroughly and regularly, making sure the soil is moist.

Nutrient Deficiency

- **Recognize:** Notice yellowing or stunted growth in plants.
- **Action:** Add organic fertilizers or compost to top up the nutrients in the soil.

Sunburn

- **Recognize:** See brown, dry patches on leaves or stems.
- **Action:** Set up shade for the plant during the hottest parts of the day.

Poor Soil

- **Recognize:** The soil is dry, hard, or dull.
- **Action:** Add compost or organic matter to improve soil quality.

Poor Pollination

- **Recognize:** Observe small or weirdly shaped fruits or flowers falling off.
- **Action:** Attract pollinators like bees by planting flowers or using bee-friendly sprays.

Improper Pruning

- **Recognize:** Notice uneven or damaged branches on plants.
- **Action:** Use clean pruning shears to properly trim plants. Be sure to know where to cut each plant. If you are unsure, ask an adult for help.

Seasonal Challenges

Each season brings its own unique obstacles, from unpredictable weather to nasty pests. Still, as always, there's nothing to worry about because, with some knowledge and clever tricks, you can breeze through these challenges and have a successful garden all year round.

Spring

- **Challenge:** Unpredictable weather and temperature changes.

- **What to Do:** Start planting seeds indoors or in a greenhouse before taking them outside. Protect young plants from cold snaps by covering them with a special cloth or plastic cover. Move potted plants indoors if you are expecting frost.

Summer
- **Challenge**: Hot temperatures and a lack of water.
- **What to Do:** Water your plants deeply and regularly; it is best to water in the early morning or evening when it's cooler. Put a layer of mulch (like straw or wood chips) around your plants to help keep the soil moist. Make shade for your plants using umbrellas or a temporary shade cloth.

Fall
- **Challenge**: Shorter days and cooler weather.
- **What to Do:** Plant cool-season crops like lettuce, spinach, and kale that like the cooler temperatures. Harvest ripe fruits and vegetables before the first frost. Use covers or plastic tunnels to protect plants from frost and keep them growing longer.

Winter
- **Challenge:** Freezing temperatures and frost.
- **What to Do:** Bring potted plants indoors or into a greenhouse to keep them warm. Put a layer of mulch around the base of plants to protect their roots. Consider planting cold-hardy vegetables like carrots that can survive the cold.

All Seasons
- **Challenge**: Weeds and pests.
- **What to Do:** Pull out weeds regularly by grabbing them at the root. Attract helpful insects like ladybugs and praying mantises by planting flowers they like. Use natural pest control methods like planting certain plants together or using friendly bugs to eat the bad bugs.

Preventive Measures in Gardening

Being a gardener is more than putting seeds in the ground and watching them grow. A gardener also cares for their plants and ensures they are healthy and happy. Just like you visit the doctor for check-ups, your plants need regular health checks, too. By performing routine garden health checks, you can look for signs of trouble or damage to your plants and take action to keep them alive. Here are some inspection routines you should practice as a good gardener:

Daily Visual Inspection
- Look closely at your plants every day.
- Check for any wilting or drooping leaves, which could mean the plant needs water.
- Look for any holes or bite marks on the leaves, which may indicate pests.

Leaf Color Check
- Examine the color of the leaves.
- Healthy leaves should be green and vibrant.
- If you see yellowing, browning, or spots on the leaves, it could be a sign of a problem.

Stem and Branch Check
- Check the stems and branches of your plants.
- Look for any cracks, breaks, or signs of damage.
- Make sure the stems and branches are strong and do not bend or droop too much.

Flower and Fruit Inspection
- Look at the flowers and fruits on your plants.
- Check if they are developing properly and not wilting or falling off prematurely.
- Look for any signs of discoloration, spots, or mold on the flowers or fruits.

Soil Moisture Test
- Gently touch the soil around your plants with your finger.
- Check if it feels dry or too wet. Plants need moist soil, not soggy or bone-dry soil.

Pest Patrol
- Keep an eye out for any bugs or insects on your plants.
- Look for small crawling creatures or flying insects around the leaves or soil.

- If you spot any pests, take note and ask an adult for help identifying and dealing with them.

Weed Control

- Scan your garden for any unwanted plants (weeds) growing among your plants.
- Pull out any weeds you find by gently tugging them from the base.
- Make sure to remove the entire weed, including the roots.

Effective Gardening Tips

Regular Gardening Maintenance

- **Tip:** Take care of your garden regularly to keep it healthy.
- **What to Do:** Remove weeds, dead leaves, and debris from your garden beds. Prune plants to remove dead or damaged branches. Keep an eye out for pests, and take action as soon as possible if you see any.

Record Keeping

- **Tip:** Keep a record of your garden activities and observations.
- **What to Do:** Use a notebook or a gardening journal to write down important information like planting dates, plant varieties, and any changes you notice in your plants. This will help you track progress and learn from your experiences.

Soil Testing

Checking your soil's health can help you ensure your plants get the right nutrients.
Photo by Roman Synkevych on Unsplash https://unsplash.com/photos/green-plant-sprouting-at-daytime-fjj7lVpCxRE

- **Tip:** Check your soil's health to ensure your plants have the right nutrients.
- **What to Do:** Use a soil testing kit or take a sample to a lab for testing. It will help you understand if your soil needs any amendments, like adding compost or fertilizer, to make it better for your plants.

Watering Techniques
- **Tip:** Water your plants properly to give them the right amount of moisture.
- **What to Do:** Use a watering can or a hose with a gentle spray nozzle. Water the base of the plants, avoiding the leaves. Water deeply but less frequently, allowing the soil to dry out slightly between waterings. This encourages plants to develop strong roots.

Composting
- **Tip:** Turn your kitchen scraps into nutrient-rich compost for your garden.
- **What to Do:** Collect fruit and vegetable scraps, coffee grounds, and eggshells. Put them in a compost bin or pile. Add some leaves, grass clippings, or shredded paper. Turn the pile occasionally. Over time, it will break down into compost that you can use to feed your soil.

Planting for Pollinators
- **Tip:** Help bees and butterflies by planting flowers they love.
- **What to Do:** Choose colorful flowers like zinnias, cosmos, and coneflowers that attract pollinators. Plant them in your garden or in pots on your balcony or windowsill. In no time, you'll be getting a lot of beautiful, helpful visitors.

Organic Gardening Methods

Organic gardening is a way of growing plants and food without using any synthetic (fake) chemicals like pesticides and fertilizers. Instead, it focuses on using natural methods to care for plants and create a healthy ecosystem in the garden. This is good because it protects the environment, keeps you healthy, and supports the balance of nature. Here are some quick and easy organic gardening methods to get you on your way to becoming an eco-friendly gardener:

Companion Planting
- **Tip:** Some plants make great friends with each other and help each other grow.
- **What to Do:** Plant certain flowers, herbs, or vegetables together to protect each other from pests or provide mutual benefits. For example, plant marigolds near tomatoes to keep pests away or grow basil near tomatoes to increase root growth, plant size, and production. Planting thyme near strawberries can increase the chances of a good harvest. Thyme is an herb that attracts bees.

    Remember: Bees are important for pollinating strawberry flowers. Sunflowers and pumpkins are another good combination. Sunflowers are tall and can provide shade for pumpkin plants, which helps keep the soil cool and moist. These are just a few examples, but many other companion plants can be grown together. Try to experiment and observe how different plants can help each other, and you might just discover something you could teach other gardeners.

Use Neem Oil
- **Tip:** Neem oil is a natural way to keep bugs away from your plants.
- **What to Do**: To make neem oil spray for plants, you'll need neem oil, mild liquid soap (like dish soap), and water. Mix 1 teaspoon of neem oil and 1/2 teaspoon of mild liquid soap in a small container. The soap helps the oil mix with water. Get a spray bottle and fill it with 4 cups of water. Pour the neem oil and soap mixture into the spray bottle. Close the spray bottle tightly and shake it well to mix everything together. Spray this mixture on the leaves, stems, and other plant parts with bugs. Make sure to spray all over the plants, including the tops and bottoms of the leaves. This spray will help eliminate bugs like aphids, mites, whiteflies, and caterpillars. Use the spray every 7-14 days or when you see bugs coming back.

Chapter Eight: Fun Garden Projects

Gardening can be a hands-on adventure that lets you actively engage with the garden and have a blast, but only if you are open to the possibilities. So many fun garden projects will spark your creativity, teach you new things, and bring a new kind of life to your outdoor space. See these projects as quests where you get to create, explore, and learn from nature. There's so much more to gardening than you expect! From creating garden art to building a bug hotel, each project will offer a unique opportunity to get your hands dirty, tap into your imagination, and work closely with the natural world.

Creating Garden Art

Use pebbles to create garden art.
Sri2161k, CC BY-SA 4.0 <https://creativecommons.org/licenses/by-sa/4.0>, via Wikimedia Commons: https://commons.wikimedia.org/wiki/File:Pebbles_6.jpg

Materials Needed:
- Smooth rocks or pebbles
- Acrylic paint
- Paintbrushes
- Sealant (optional)
- Clear varnish or outdoor Mod Podge (optional)

Instructions:
1. **Collect Rocks**: Go on a hunt for smooth rocks or pebbles of different sizes and shapes. Make sure they are clean and dry before starting.
2. **Design Ideas:** Think about what kind of garden art you want to create. It could be ladybugs, flowers, or even colorful patterns.
3. **Paint Your Rocks:** Lay out a protective surface, like a newspaper or a tablecloth. Using acrylic paint to bring your design ideas to life, apply a base coat on the rock, and then add details and colors to create your desired design. Don't forget to let each layer of paint dry before adding more.
4. **Decorate Your Garden**: Once your painted rocks are completely dry, it's time to display them in your garden. Find the best spot where you want to add some garden art. You can place them in a flower bed, a garden path, or a potted plant. Arrange the rocks in a way that makes the beauty of your garden pop and brings a touch of creativity to the space.
5. **Seal the Artwork (Adult Supervision Required)**: Apply a sealant to protect your garden art from the weather. Ask an adult to help you with this step. Use a clear varnish or outdoor Mod Podge to seal the painted rocks. Apply a thin, even layer, and let it dry completely.
6. **Enjoy and Learn:** Observe how your garden art enhances the total beauty of your garden. Take note of any changes or reactions from insects or birds that visit your garden art. Learn about different insects or animals that may be attracted to your art and their role in the ecosystem.

Setting Up a Theme Garden

Designing a theme garden is a fun way to create a garden space with plants that have a specific message or story. It's very easy, and anyone can do it. To get started:

1. **Choose a Theme:** The first step is to pick a theme for your garden. It could be anything you like, from butterflies, dinosaurs, and fairies to even your favorite book or movie. Just think about what you love and what makes you excited.

2. **Research Your Theme:** Once you have a theme in mind, do some research to learn more about it. Look for books and websites, or ask an adult for help. Find out what kinds of plants, colors, and decorations are associated with your theme.

3. **Plan Your Garden:** Draw a simple garden layout on a piece of paper. Think about where you want to put different plants and decorations. Remember to leave enough space for your plants to grow.

4. **Choose Plants:** Now, it's time to pick the plants that go with your theme. For example, if you have chosen a butterfly theme, you could plant flowers that attract butterflies, like lavender or coneflowers. If you have chosen a dinosaur theme, you could go with leafy plants that give off a prehistoric jungle vibe. Kale, lettuce, and basil are good examples.

5. **Add Some Decorations:** Decorations can make your theme garden even more realistic. You can make your own decorations using craft materials or find ready-made ones at a store. For example, if you choose a fairy theme, you could add some small fairy statues or a mini fairy house.

6. **Plant and Care for Your Garden:** Now it's time to start planting. Follow the instructions on the plant tags or ask an adult for help. Make sure to water your plants regularly and give them enough sunlight. Weeds can compete with your plants for water and nutrients, so you must keep an eye out for them and remove them when you see them.

Garden Projects

The garden projects you'll find here are not only fun, but they also teach you important concepts. Here are some projects that will add a bit of knowledge to your gardening experience:

Water Cycle Project

The water cycle explains how water moves around the Earth. You can learn about it by creating your own mini-water cycle in a jar. Here's how:

1. Find a clear glass jar and fill it about one-third full with water.
2. Place a small plate or plastic wrap on top of the jar, making sure it's tightly sealed.
3. Put the jar in a sunny spot, like a windowsill, and watch what happens over a few days.
4. As the sun heats the water, the water evaporates, and you'll see water droplets forming on the bottom of the plate or plastic wrap. The droplets are the result of a process called condensation and symbolize the clouds.
5. After a while, the droplets will fall and return to the water in the jar, symbolizing rain falling from the clouds. This part of the cycle is called *precipitation.*

This project shows how water evaporates from the earth's surface, forms clouds, and then returns as rain, completing the water cycle.

Butterfly Life Cycle Project

Butterflies go through a fascinating transformation called metamorphosis. You can learn about their life cycle by creating a butterfly garden and observing their stages. Here's what you can do:

1. Find a sunny spot in your garden or a large pot and fill it with soil.
2. Plant some butterfly-friendly flowers like milkweed, which is food for caterpillars, and other nectar-rich flowers like zinnias or marigolds.
3. Look for butterfly eggs or caterpillars on the milkweed leaves. If you find any, gently place them in a jar with some leaves.
4. Watch the caterpillars as they eat and grow. They will molt (shed their skin) several times and get bigger.

5. Once they stop eating and get bigger, they will form a chrysalis, a protective covering made of silk.
6. Keep watching the chrysalis; after some time, you'll notice a beautiful butterfly come out of it.
7. Release the butterfly in your garden. Watch it fly around, and enjoy the flowers.

By observing the butterfly's life cycle, you'll learn about their different stages, from an egg to a caterpillar, then a chrysalis, and finally a butterfly.

How to Interact with Garden Wildlife

Interacting with garden wildlife is exciting, but if you're going to do it, you must do it right.

Bird Feeders

A bird feeder can help you interact with garden wildlife.
https://unsplash.com/photos/brown-bird-on-red-wooden-bird-house-vkDh08uoNJg?utm_content=creditShareLink&utm_medium=referral&utm_source=unsplash

1. Find a sturdy plastic bottle or an empty milk carton.
2. Ask an adult to help you cut a small hole near the bottom of the bottle or carton.
3. Decorate the bottle or carton with colorful paint or markers.

4. Punch two small holes near the top and thread a string through them to hang the feeder.
5. Fill the feeder with birdseed or small pieces of fruit.
6. Hang it in a tree or on a pole in your garden.
7. Watch from a distance and enjoy seeing different birds visit your feeder.

Bug Hotel
1. Get a small wooden box or container with a lid.
2. Decorate the box if you want to make it look pretty.
3. Make different levels and rooms inside the box using sticks, twigs, and branches.
4. Put pine cones, bamboo, or hollow reeds in some rooms for insects to hide and lay eggs.
5. Fill other rooms with dry leaves or straws to create spaces for insects to rest.
6. Find a quiet spot in your garden to place the tiny house.
7. Dig a shallow hole and partly bury the box, leaving the entrance accessible. Or use a string or wire to secure the box to a tree branch or stake.
8. Check the tiny house regularly and add new materials when needed.
9. Watch and learn about the insects that visit the tiny house.
10. Don't use any harmful chemicals in your garden to keep the insects safe.

Garden Games

Here are some fun garden-based games and activities you can enjoy with your family and friends.

Scavenger Hunt
1. Make a list of items that can be found in the garden, like a particular leaf, a flower, a rock, or a feather.
2. Give each player a copy of the list and a bag to collect their treasures.
3. Set a timer and see who can find all the items on the list first.

Nature Bingo
1. Create bingo cards with pictures of things you might find in the garden, such as a ladybug, a butterfly, a tree, or a bird.
2. Give each player a bingo card and a pen or marker.
3. Explore the garden together and mark off the items on your card as you spot them.
4. The first person to get a line or a full card marked off yells, "Bingo!" and wins the game.

Garden Obstacle Course
1. Set up a fun obstacle course in your garden using objects you find, like hula hoops, cones, or jump ropes.
2. Create challenges like hopping through hoops, zig-zagging between cones, or balancing on a log.
3. Time each player as they complete the course and see who can finish it the fastest.

Thank You Message

Thank you for choosing this book and taking an interest in gardening. Your efforts and enthusiasm in exploring the world of gardening are impressive. Seeing your love for nature blossoming and your skills and knowledge growing alongside it is amazing. Your curiosity and willingness to learn are enough to truly inspire everyone else around you!

As you went through this book, you discovered the pure magic behind watching a tiny seed transform into a beautiful flower or the healthiest vegetable. You've learned about the importance of sunshine, water, and soil for your plants. You've seen how gardening can light up your day and give you something to look forward to.

The garden is a place filled with endless possibilities. It's a means to connect with the natural world, care for plants, and create your own little piece of paradise. It is not just about growing pretty flowers or edible greens. It's a celebration of nature and all the amazing creatures that work together to keep the natural world alive. It is about taking care of the environment.

You'll be an amazing gardener! Always remember the positive and encouraging message this book carries. Don't stop being curious about the wonderful world of gardening. Nature is waiting for you to discover all her secrets through your love for plants and animals. Your skills and experience will grow just like the flowers in a garden because you can do incredible things. Believe in yourself, go out there, and let your green thumbs lead the way!

Here's another book by Dion Rosser that you might like

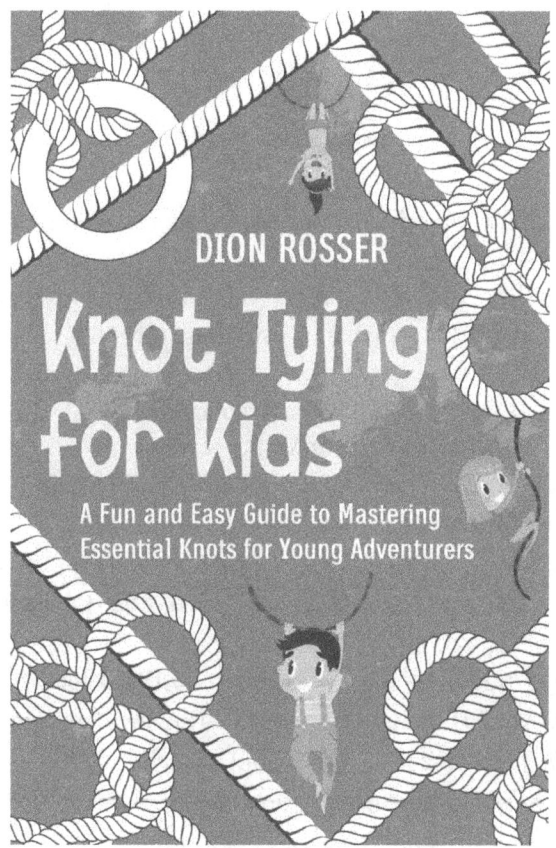

References

Alsuwaidi, N. A. (2017, March 20). Little Gardener. Createspace Independent Publishing Platform.

Bone, E., & Wheatley, A. (2015, January 1). Gardening for Beginners.

Collins, C., & Lia, L. (2017, April 4). Grow Your Own for Kids. Mitchell Beazley.

Cutler, K. D., Fisher, K., DeJohn, S., & Association, N. G. (2010, October 29). Herb Gardening For Dummies. John Wiley & Sons.

Flint, M. L. (2018, January 1). Pests of the Garden and Small Farm, 3rd Edition. UCANR Publications.

Gaines, J. (2019, March 26). We Are the Gardeners. Thomas Nelson.

Gosling, L. (2023, February 28). My First Garden. DK Publishing (Dorling Kindersley).

Hogner, D. C. (1974, January 1). Good Bugs and Bad Bugs in Your Garden.

Krezel, C. (2010, April 1). Kids' Container Gardening. Chicago Review Press.

Lovejoy, S. (2017, January 24). Roots, Shoots, Buckets & Boots. Hachette UK.

Pierce, T. (2019, May 7). My Busy Green Garden.

Tai, L. (2021, March 15). The Magic of Children's Gardens. Temple University Press

www.ingramcontent.com/pod-product-compliance
Lightning Source LLC
Chambersburg PA
CBHW051843160426
43209CB00006B/1135